The Collected Poems
1972 - 2016

Graham A. Rhodes.

First Edition
Templar Publishing, Scarborough 2016

First published 2016
Templar Publishing, Scarborough, England

Copyright Graham A. Rhodes

Conditions of Sale.

This book is sold subject to the condition that it shall not, by way of trade or otherwise, be lent, re-sold, hired out, or otherwise circulated without the publisher's prior consent, in any form of binding or cover other than that in which it is published.

All rights reserved. No part of this publication may be reproduced, stored in a retrieval system, or transmitted, in any form or by any means, electronic, mechanical, photocopying, recording or otherwise, without the prior permission of the publishers and copyright holder. Otherwise, you get your pee pee slapped!

Cover photograph –
Graham Rhodes, Aakschipper Images

Acknowledgements

You expect a book like this to have acknowledgements so I'm not going to disappoint you. Some are friends, some acquaintances, and some I've never met, but over the years all of them have in some way influenced what you are about to read. It gets a bit long but when you are putting together a lifetimes worth of poetry there's a lot to acknowledge. So here goes. With love and thanks to - Tommy Simpson, Nick Jones, Gordon Davison, Dave Pruckner, Dennis Appleyard, Stuart Pearson, Phil Finch, Kev & Bonk, Andi Lee, John Cooper Clarke, Mike Hardin, John Middleton, Wally, Kinky Friedman, Paul Simon, Roger McGough, Ogden Nash, Roy Harper, Seahouse, Velma, Captain Beefheart, Frank Zappa, Randy California, John Stewart, Thomas Pynchon, Eric Gill, Alan Garner, Gary Barrett (& Life Support & Stone Cold Sober), Bandanna, Aldo & His Orphans, Martin, Nigel & Wayne, Hardliners all, Vivian Stanshill, Will Hay, Compton Mackenzie, Dylan Thomas, Groucho Marx, Max Miller, Ian Dury, Billy Bennett, Marriott Edgar, Bob Williamson, Fibbers, John Otway, Tim Minchin, Peter Tinniswood, Raymond E. Feist, David Eddings, Terry Pratchett, Bill Hicks, Denis Leary, Sister Gregory, Madge & Lawrence Rhodes, Samantha Rhodes, Jesse Hutchinson, The Baytown Rattlers, Eli & The Blues Prophets, Toby Jepson, Yvonne, Frankie & Heather (& Granddad), Richard, Chris, The Badgers Of Bohemia, Jo, Tubbs & Missy, Lucy, Magenta, Anna Shannon & all at The Cellars, & finally Ysanne in the hope that one day it will turn up in her bookshop.

Introduction

No, I'm not telling you how old I am. Suffice it to say that for something like forty years I worked at the creation of visual communications. So let me own up here and now. Yes, I did help to launch Monster Munch on an unsuspecting world, along with Kestrel Lager and Scampi Fries. Yes, I did help to create the product launch for the Ford Sierra, the Volvo 454, and other various Rover cars. Yes, I did design product for such bands as The Police, Squeeze, and The Cramps. But these were the high spots. My other less known claims to fame involved working for long forgotten bands and products whose nose dive into oblivion was even more spectacular. Products like Apricot Computers, Farmer Browns and Battle Bags, bands like Ghost Dance, Skafish, Raw-Ho, Mickey Drury and the Sirens. I mean, do you remember the "Boogie till you Puke" campaign for Root Boy Slim and the Sex Change Band? - God, I wish I didn't!

In the course of my career I have found myself down coal mines, in printing plants, on board ships, in planes, riding on the footplate of steam engines, standing on the top of London's Nat West Tower, poking around in the ancient ruins of towns like London, Colchester, Leeds and York, and have walked around more factory floors and seen more manufacturing processes than you can shake the proverbial stick at. In the course of this work I have met many good people, many talented people, some famous people and many extraordinary people. I have also met more than my fair share of assholes.

All these things leave mental scars and tend to jaundice one's view of life, that and being a lifelong supporter of Leeds United! The following poems are a result of that jaundiced view.

Many of these poems are the ones I perform on rock 'n roll stages in various pubs and clubs. Others have now slipped out of my live act, but still deserve to see the light of day. Some may cause raised eyebrows, some might even cause offence to the weak hearted. If so I apologise in advance, that is not their intention. They are written to make you laugh, or cry, but mostly think.
I hope you enjoy them.

Graham Rhodes
Scarborough 2016.

The Collected Poems
1972 - 2016

This is one of the earliest poems I wrote that I still occasionally perform. I can remember writing it on a train travelling from Leeds to Harrogate which must have been when I moved to Harrogate circa 1970/71.

Horace the Pigeon

Once upon a time, far out in t' Dales
there was this here pigeon called Horace,
now Horace being an unusual sort of pigeon
thought he'd like to see more of the world,
so he flew down Aire Valley
looking at Keighley, Shipley, and Bingley
but, as he didn't reckon much to them
passed onto Leeds and Hunslet,
and thought he were in some sort of Hell.

Now Horace flew round in a circle,
cos all grim and all soot and all muck
had clogged up most of his feathers,
and he were feeling reet out of luck.

Till at last he came into Bradford,
at least he assumed he were there
cos a dollup of summat got him reet in t'eye
and he couldn't see owt at all.

Then suddenly CRASH,
and with a bloody great Splat,
he flew into t'town hall wall
and poor Horace was sadly demised.

This story was told with sheer horror,
by pigeons from far and from wide,
and that's why if you're ever in Bradford,
and you take a peep up into skies,
all pigeons are flying arse forward,
to keep bloody muck from their eyes.

I Was a Teenage Werewolf is a 1957 horror film starring Michael Landon as a troubled teenager, and Whit Bissell as the primary adult. Back in the day I did some graphic design work for a great band called The Cramps. "I Was A Teenage Werewolf" was also track on their album "Songs The Lord Taught Us." This is my homage to both of them.

I Was a Teenage Werewolf

I was a teenage werewolf
who always knew his place
I drank my soup before it clotted
and always combed my face

Bella Lugosi in Levis
with a toothy sort of grin
the only teenager in our street
to wear Brylcreem on his chin

I drank virgin's blood
with ice and lemon
my face has been hairy
since I was seven

I used to howl at the neighbour's wife
till she attacked me with a silver bread knife
and the postman wears a garlic clove
when he delivers down our road

I tried to learn the piano
I practised every night
but gave it up when I realised
my Bach was worse than my bite

Getting a job was never easy
at interviews I shrank
I got turned down for a job
at our local blood bank

But after some years on the dole
I got a job at last
teaching young conservatives
to suck blood from the working class.

I suppose this could be a case of hypocrisy as in the late 90's I wrote dialogue and storylines for some rather good computer games. However as this is a poem on how you shouldn't allow computer games to take over your life I think I'm OK.

Techno Freaking Anorak

Train spotter of the nineties in his virtual techno dream
nose pressed tightly up against his blue computer screen

By day he presses buttons on his company's Apple Mac
at night he's flying spaceships from his terraced back to back.

At weekends he goes surfing, along the internet
his wife and kids have left him, but he hasn't noticed yet

He talks to people in Hong Kong and people in New York
blocking up the hyper space with his boring anorak talk

his fingers move like maggots over keyboard and his mouse
it's his only form of exercise now he never leaves the house

his arse is getting bigger cos he never leaves his chair
his real life's gone to ruin but he doesn't really care

he's into sword and sorcery, and silly role play games
it's never really hit him that they're all the bloody same

and sex is not a problem now porn's on CD-Rom
despite his body weakening, his wrist is getting strong

he thinks it's bloody marvellous fighting simulated war
he'd like to play it with his mates but they don't come round no more

he thinks his life is wonderful playing computer simulated strife
I've just one thing to say to him, that's get a bloody life

go out and go enjoy yourself in pub or club or boozer
don't let life pass you by as a sad computer loser.

At first the lottery was a bit of a jokey gamble, a harmless bit of fun then, as austerity has kicked in, it seems as if some politicians want to use it to fund the NHS, the Arts and other things that our taxes should be paying for. That is not funny. I haven't brought it up to date and still keep the name of John Major in it but feel free to substitute the names Cameron, or May in there. It really makes no difference.

Lottery

The lottery's a mockery
just another kind of drug
designed as entertainment
treating people as real mugs

religion is the opium
of the people, said Karl Marx
now the revolution's cancelled
just give them all scratch cards

It's getting out of hand
all this scratch and win
The good old Church of England
proclaimed scratch cards as a sin

It's a sin they take our money
It's a sin we never win
It's a sin they need the income
to pay for everything

that should be paid by government
from the proceeds of our tax
not feathering the pockets
of fat rich city cats

Camelot makes billions
from the likes of me and you
but still the homeless huddle
in cardboard boxes at Waterloo

They've privatised just everything
that belonged to you and me
they've sold the country under us
to prop up the economy

I've a message for John Major
in Westminster greed filled halls
meet me under the pawnbrokers sign
and kiss me under the balls.

This was written as an answer to the criticism once levelled at me that I never write love poems. I think it speaks for itself.

A Love Poem

Tonight I lit a rocket
it shot towards the moon
stars fell down like diamonds
I always come too soon!

I live in Scarborough and every so often I walk along the seafront and pass the amusement arcades. Outside two of these arcades there are two identical mechanical Eastern mystics, both called Zoltar and both speak to you as you walk past. I like them and this is a daft little poem dedicated to them both.

Zoltar

Zoltar tells the future
He lives inside a box
You only see him from waist up
That's why he wears no socks

Zoltar tells your future
For only fifty pee
But can you trust a forecast
From someone with no knees

Zoltar tells your future
Whether good or whether bad
His wooden voice intones your fate
That's why he looks so sad

Zoltar tells your future
And Zoltar never smiles
He sits outside inside his box
That's why he suffers piles

Zoltars eyes are mechanical
Zoltar knows your fate
Zoltar knows if you've got time
But he knows that it's too late

Zoltar knows your future
From deep inside his box
And all the time he's planning
On how to steal your socks

And sometime in the night time
When the amusements all shut down
Zoltar puts his legs back on
And stalks around the town

So beware the darkened alleys
Beware deserted docks
In case Zoltar tries to grab you
Knock you down and steal your socks.

I wrote this back in the late seventies and never performed it in public until the recent hundred year commemoration of World War I. Originally the poem was meant to imply that the gap in the bed between separating lovers was a sort of no man's land. Now after tracing my own Grandfathers journey through Ypres, Mons and the Somme it takes on a deeper meaning.

No Man's land

The trees are restless here tonight
they shake beneath the cannons might
and as the shells thump in the mud
The army smells the stench of blood

Beneath the two divisions stands
The emptiness of no man's land
Where bullets whine and dead men lie
In no man's land you'll hear no cry

In no man's land nobody strays
In no man's land there are no days
In no man's land there are no nights
In no man's land there's just the fright

The rags of once proud uniforms
Are buried under fields of corn
The poppies all sing out in red
They mourn the buried and the dead

Every man fears no man's land
Where no ones near to hold a hand
When daylight turns into gloom
No man's land is one small room

And every lover passed and gone
Has heard the muffled pipe and drum
They know they have to make a stand
And walk alone through no man's land

Now once proud love has passed away
Like soldiers faded into clay
Alone they walk with empty hands
To lose themselves in no man's land

This was written back in the 1990's as a protest to spending money on fads and trends specially designed to part parents from their money, which were all created by advertising men with big budgets.

Miserable Bastard

I ate "Babe" for breakfast
with tomatoes and a slice
a portion of beans and two fried eggs,
it tasted really nice.

I see the final film's been made
by Nick Parks the animator
when Wallace and Gromit got left overnight
on the studio radiator

I don't believe in fairy tales
especially ads by bankers.
Get an overdraft by telephone,
don't treat us all like wankers!

Nice and twee is marketing speak
for profits and corporate greed
it's used to sell us plastic crap
and things that we don't need

Like "My Little Pony" stable blocks
and model thunderbirds
Power rangers and Barbie dolls
and Mutant Ninja Turtles

Some think that stuff like that's alright
some people think it's funny
you might think I'm a miserable bastard
but I'd rather keep hold of my money

I'm wary of all those adverts
that peddle useless trash
it's the really useless products
that have adverts big and flash

The power of the Ad man
don't think it doesn't matter
'cos they're the slimy cretins
that sold us Margaret Thatcher.

This poem follows on the same sort of rant only specifically aimed at those Furbie creatures that, back in the 90's, no home was complete without one.

Furbie

I got a Furbie for Christmas
And I crucified the twat on Boxing Day
But that tiny ball of fluff
was made of sterner stuff
Cos the fucker rose again on New Years Day.

I got a Furbie for Christmas
and by Boxing Day I'd nailed it to the wall
that furry little shit
nearly made me lose my wits
with its whimpering and its bloody awful drawl.

It started off the moment I unpacked it
When it belched - and then it farted in my hand
So I dropped it to the ground
And kicked the fucker round
But the thing was in my life and I was damned

"Furbie wants a cuddle!" said the monster
so I poked it in both eyes with me fountain pen
the little shit just blinked,
and I'll swear it gave a wink
as it asked me "Please do not do that to me again!"

The bloody thing just wouldn't stop its talking
And a Furbie has no switch to turn it off
So I began a close inspection
with plans to start dissection
but thing just smiled and gave a little cough

These Furbies drive me wild, there's not a woman,
man nor child
That's immune from their chattering and jabber
But I think I'll win the day
And I'll finally have my say
Cos I've just bought myself a shiny nice new hammer.

I can't remember when I wrote this, or why. I do know that it's been a constant poem in my live act since the early nineteen nineties though. I like name-checking the stars of children's TV as the older I get the more I try to spot the members of the audience that remember them as well. Mind you with YouTube it seems that some of them live on in the hearts and minds of today's children – so perhaps Bagpuss and The Herbs will never die. I rather hope so.

Heroes

What happened to all of my heroes
to Parsley, to Dill and to Sage
do they still live in that garden
all wrinkled and twisted with age?

Whatever happened to Dougal?
Was Zebedee ever unscrewed?
Florence and Dylan got married
McDonalds got poor Ermintrude!

Postman Pat ran over his cat
when his van got stuck in reverse
the post office made him redundant
and now he's driving a hearse.

Whatever happened to Trumpton?
The town is deserted they say
The Halifax reclaimed their mortgage
and they all had to move far away.

Peter Rabbit got myxomatosis
Winnie the Pooh just got fat
Zippy opened a chippy
and Garfield just shat on the mat.

Privatisation hit Thomas
Noddy got stabbed by Big Ears
Bagpuss eloped with the Clangers
but it all ended sadly in tears.

Andy Pandy got busted,
heroin, crack and cocaine
Teddy became alcoholic
Looby Lou's now on the game

So don't fall for your childhood heroes
they'll all let you down just the same
they only did it for the money
for the sex and the drugs and the fame.

I think this poems shows I might have a bit of a nihilistic approach to life. It was written in the late 90's when I was in love with Anna Friel the actress that played Beth Jordache in Brookside. Oh and I've always dug the music of REM and Michael Stipe.

The End Of The World As We Know It
(With Apologies to Michael Stipe)

It's getting really dangerous
just to stay alive
whatever happened to love and peace
and all that hippy jive.

It's dangerous on the corner
it's dangerous on the street
there's always something lurking
to knock you off your feet

It's getting so that no one
really gives a damn
there's very few that give a shit
about their fellow man

everyone's out for profit
everyone wants gain
and no one gives a flying fuck
if their action causes pain

the rain is pissing down on us
the shit has hit the fan
the world is slowly ending
with a whimper, not a bang

everyone has worries
everyone has troubles
every one of us meets that giant prick
that busts all of our bubbles

someone blow the whistle
someone bang the gong
the game is really over
the fat man's sung the song

you can blame it on the government
blame it on the weather
blame it on your parents
it won't make it any better

me I blame it on the telly
I lay the blame on Channel Four
'cos since Beth walked out of Brookside
life's not worth living any more.

This is a new poem written in 2016. It does have a serious point. My gallery is on Scarborough's Pier and on daily basis I see the amount of plastic that appears on the small South Bay beach. Magnify that a million times and you get some idea of how much plastic there is out there on and I our seven seas. It is strangling seabirds and choking the life out of marine creatures, now thanks to those small plastic beads plastic have entered the food chain. There's too much of it and we need to do something, if only tidy up after us.

A Bag for Life

The handles fallen off my bag for life
It looks like it's been cut off by a knife
Is my shelf life now outdated?
Am I cursed? Am I ill-fated?
Cos the handles fallen off my bag for life

The bottoms fallen out my bag for life
I think that it's a metaphor for strife
My situations drastic
But I won't revert to plastic
My bottoms hanging out my bag for life.

Now what happens when your bag for life is dead?
This question keeps on messing up my head
My brain is in a muddle
With this philosophical type puzzle
How the fuck can you outlive your bag for life?

Another serious point, why isn't sex in the movies believable. They say that any footage featuring gratuitous violence is justified because that's how life is – therefore why don't they show sex like it really is – just saying like!

Movie Sex

Why isn't sex like it is in the movies?
How come it's always alright on the night?
How is it that all the romantic heroes
always manage to do things just right?

How can it be that Mel Gibson,
Bruce Willis, Tom Cruise and that lot
never suffer premature ejaculation
always finding their women's G-spot

How can it be that they sit there
with their drugs and their booze every day
but it never affects their performance
brewers droop can't exist in L.A.

How come they get instant erections
the moment they get into the sheets
and no one says "I'm too tired!"
and just turns and rolls over and sleeps

how come in all of the love scenes
there's never a moment when they
have to stop to pull on a condom
before they can have it away

how come in their moment of passion
there's never a tissue in sight
but there's always clean sheets and no wet patch
to roll into much later at night

how is it that all of the couples
come together so sweet and sublime
their women never lay back saying
"once again, and it's my turn this time!"

But why pay to see sex in the movies
where the stars never stop for a pee
when you can stay home at night and shag witless
cos it's the only thing left that's for free!

This was written as a celebration poem in the halcyon days when we got rid of the Tory party. When Tony Blair represented a new hope and a new face on politics. Oh dear. Just as Pete Townsend once sang, "Here comes the new boss, same as the old boss." I was and still am against his intervention in Iraq and like many others still state it was not in my name.

Eighteen Fucking Years

They couldn't sort a piss up in a brewery
but for eighteen years they fucked with you and me
those Westminster alcoholics
with their bloody gin and tonics
really screwed up our economy

but on May 1st we finally got our own back
when we really made the Tory party pay
Those bastard sons of Thatcher had it coming
it's just a pity there's no guillotine today

for eighteen bloody years they held the power
and shat upon the British working class
they've stitched us up and sold us down the river
but together we went and knocked them on their ass

for far too long we read about their scruples
the ones they said that should apply to us
whilst they drift to Chelsea flats to screw their mistress
enjoying the privilege of class

We remembered the crucifixion of the miners
the railway workers and the poorly paid
and the selling off of water and the systematic slaughter
of the unions that our fathers fought to gain

for eighteen bloody years they screwed the country
and made riches for their families and friends
with beneficial policies and market force economies
but now their sleaze filled rule is at an end

'cos when it came to voting you do it wisely
you voted green or loony, whatever was about
you voted anything you bloody had to
and finally got those sad Tory fuckers out.

This poem was originally a song called "It's Just Love" as performed by the folk group Arkwright's Ferret which I performed with circa 1977- 82. (Of which the Melody Maker once said "Steeleye Span meets Motorhead, and loses!). The original lyrics were co-written by myself and the singer "Fang". Since then I've mucked them about a bit and given them a new ending. Unfortunately, in 2014 I heard that, after many years as a busker working in Archway, Fang died. Ruth Ewan in conjunction with AIR (Archway Investigations and Responses) at the Byam Shaw School of Art, created a project called Fang Sang which offers a glimpse into his creative outputs. Here's a link - http://www.ruthewan.com/fang_sang.html

Perversion

Draw closed the curtains
turn off the light
turn off the telly
and we'll do it tonight

You wear the pac-a-mac
I'll be the Nun
slide on your wellies
and we'll have some fun

It's nothing perverted
It's nothing strange
because you like bondage
don't mean your deranged

You bite my buttocks
and I'll lose my grip
I'll lay in chains
while you use the whip

We'll go to a place
where nobody goes
you sit on the bidet
while I suck your toes

I'll paint all of my
private parts red
while you wear my underwear
over your head

You pour the treacle
and I'll lick it off
you hold my bits
while I have a cough

There's nothing perverted
it's really cool
cos I learnt these ways
from my old public school

There's nothing scary
There's nothing sinister
It's just a day in the life
of a cabinet minister.

Another poem written in the nineties and a pop at the bankers and the City – it's as well deserved now as it was then. In fact looking back over recent years, even more deserved.

City Bastards

Those bastards in the City who control our daily lives
snorting coke inside their board rooms
then drive home to screw their wives

after a session in the wine bar
with their rugger playing mates
swapping notes on who they've screwed this week -
they get home rather late

Two faced fucking weasels
with two Volvos in the drive
a Kellogs breakfast family
that's never had to strive

With their mobiles in their pockets
and their brains stuck up their bum
their electronic diary's their substitute for fun

they think they know the working class
they pass them on the street
on their way to champagne meetings
to discuss new ways to cheat

to make the shareholders happy they close another works
    they don't give a toss of the consequence
      as long as they get their perks

      as long as they have stocks and shares
      we can all go straight to hell
      they'll sell our jobs from under us
      and smile and wish us well

      they check their shite for fibre,
      they've too much leisure time
      they've all got too much money
      they've got what's yours and mine

      I've a message for the city,
    for the nobs in their suits and ties
you'll be the first against the bloody wall
      when we march to claim our rights

This poem was written at the height of Thatcher and her Tory government. It refers to passing of The Criminal Justice and Public Order Act of 1994.

Democracy

You talk about democracy
of the land of the brave and free
but the Union Jacks round the cenotaph
don't wave for you and me.

We've got no constitution,
we've got no bill of rights.
Just a vote to keep us quiet
and a knock on the door at night

But as long as we're earning money
got enough to buy a pint
we don't give a shit for anyone else
no money means no rights.

They victimise the dissident
in this land of the brave and free
today gypsies, raves, and travellers
tomorrow - you and me.

Our government relies on indolence
and we played right into their hands,
they're dancing nightly in Westminster
now they've got all the sub-cultures banned.

Government for the people by the people
don't make me want to laugh
and where were you when they fucked us
with the Criminal Justice Act?

I've moved around a lot in my life, and with each house move The Readers Digest always found me. To this day I have no idea how but as the magazine no longer exists it no longer applies, apart from now I seem to get even more junk mail.

Angst

You can change your name by deed poll,
you can move and change address.
You can wear false beards and moustache,
you can even wear a dress.

You try changing your identity
you can run but you can't hide
cos those bastards know you're out there
and they'll chase you till you die.

From Ilfracombe to Southport
from Glasgow down to Staines,
in every street in every town
they know all of our names.

They know everything about us
we're on their database.
Our lives are just statistics
we're just numbers with no face

you can move from town to country,
you can move from house to flat,
but before you even get there
its laying on the mat.

There's no way of escaping them,
they're such a bloody pain.
Those letters from Readers Digest
always signed by Tom Champagne.

This poem has been around for ages. I first did it in the late seventies with Arkwright's Ferret. To keep it updated I've just altered the name at the end. Over the years there's been no shortage of people to add in there.

This Is Not a Love Poem

You've got a mouth like the River Humber
Your skin is like green cheese
Your nose is like a 747
That's crashed between your knees

You're like a nosebleed at a party
that dripped in the kids ice cream
You're like summat that festered overnight
and woke up looking horribly obscene

You're like a tramp that been evicted
from a bin in a council bog
You're like a door to door Mormon
That's been bitten by a dog

You're like vomit in a puddle
on a newly polished floor.
Like the leper that threw his hand in
I don't want to know you no more

You're an evil minded harridan
You're a blot on the rest of mankind
You're a boil on the devils bottom
You're what makes Venetian's blind

You spread disease like butter
You breath transmits foul air
Your brains like a nest of maggots
You make me want to swear

You're like a cannibal on a health food trip
eating only vegetarians
I hope to god you don't survive
To be an octogenarian

What kind of creature bore you?
Was it some sort of bat?
Cos you're names Katie Hopkins
And you're a vicious, racist twat.

I've never really enjoyed participating in sports. At school I got my nose broken twice, once by a fast bowler and then by the entire front row of an opposing rugby team hitting me as I tried to catch a ball and I hated cross country running with a vengeance. However I do like watching, preferably from a bar. I'm an observer not a participant, but there again, I suppose that's what writers do.

Sports

You can stuff your sports activities
sideways up your arse
I don't want to know about anything
involving balls and grass

I can't stand golf, hate playing tennis
I don't want to jog or run
physical exertions
not my idea of fun

Cricket, football, rugby
are for watching on TV
with a couple of spliffs and a pack of six
resting on your knee

Ian Dury said it best
when he wrote that song
with sex and drugs and rock 'n roll
you really can't go wrong

Sex and drugs and rock 'n roll
that order isn't fixed
sometimes I have rock 'n roll
then have drugs and sex

No matter what the order
it doesn't really matter
cos sex and drugs and rock 'n roll
won't make you any fatter

Faster - Higher - Stronger
marks Olympian respect
it's also what we long for
from rock 'n roll, drugs and sex

This poem has been around for a long while. It was originally called "The Bloody Orkneys", written by someone called Captain Hamish Blair and appeared in the book "Verse and Worse" first published by Faber & Faber in 1952. It was one of the first pieces of writing that turned me onto the possibilities of the power of poetry. John Cooper Clarke found it and re-arranged it so that it appeared as "Evidently Chickentown" on his 1980 album "Snap Crackle & Bop", Epic Records EPC84083. This is my interpretation of the same theme. The sad thing about is that for over fifty years the same complaints can be levied at the rural areas of Britain, but then does that really come as a surprise?

Rural England

All bloody clouds
and bloody rain
no bloody sun
no bloody drains
the councils got no bloody brains
in rural England

This bloody place
is a bloody pain
no bloody bus
no bloody train
the council sold them all for gain
in rural England

the filling station
has no gas
everything's
put out to grass
it seems the 20th century's passed
by rural England

The bloody shops
are bloody shut
the bloody pubs
a bloody hut
there's only one man and his mut
left in rural England

the bloody roads
are bloody bad
the bloody people
bloody mad
everyone's so bloody sad
in rural England

Best bloody place
is bloody bed
with bloody sheets
pulled over head
you might as well be bloody dead
in rustic England

This is self explanatory. I just liked the idea of putting as many TV detectives into a poem as possible.

Detectives

They seek him here, they seek him there
they're looking for the fucker everywhere

Cracker, Maigret, Sherlock Holmes
looking down rabbit holes, lifting up stones

Colombo, Ironside and The Bill
can't find any trace of him.

Bergerac, and Hawaii 5
couldn't bring him back alive

Brodrick Crawford & Highway Patrol
couldn't find a trace at all

LA Law and Hill Street Blues
couldn't pick up any clues

Taggert, Frost, and Mulder & Scully
found his disappearance funny

Lord Peter Whimsey and Scotland Yard
have even found the going hard

The best detectives in all the world
couldn't turn up any word

He's the missing person they couldn't trace
he too ashamed to show his face

It brought an end to all their glory
cos they can't find the shit that voted Tory.

Euphemisms and innuendo are the stuff of British humour a la Carry on Movies. I wrote this after Manchester Utd. won the 1996 FA Cup when Eric Cantona, playing as captain, scored the only goal in the 86th minute. I'm not really a Man Utd fan but I am a huge Eric Cantona fan, and if you want to know why just check out Ken Loach's brilliant 2009 movie "Looking For Eric."

Footysex

For over an hour they parried and thrust
feeling each other, sensing the lust.

They had reputations that had gone on before
both of them had scored many times before.

They were both experienced, they'd both played around
they started their game with their feet on the ground.

They both played at home, and then had it away
they knew they'd end up with each other one day.

They toyed with each other all afternoon
hoping each other would give in quite soon.

They both pushed forward, they moved end to end
till their legs grew tired and their knees sagged and bent

They forced through the middle, it went up so gently
then they pushed it about, in an increase of frenzy.

They stroked it around from side to side
as one of them moaned and the other one sighed.

Then Cantona struck and the ball went straight in
Man U. won the Cup - one goal to nil

This is another poem that features strongly in my live act. All poems are autobiographical and this is about bad luck combined with my support for a certain football team.

Unlucky Sad Bastard

Life's a drag - I'm right pissed off
I'm buggered if I know what to do.
My silver cloud is hiding
my world's flushed down the loo.

The rain is falling on me head
it's always lousy weather.
I've had so much bad luck
the gipsy took back her heather.

When my ship came in
I was waiting for a plane,
the buggeration factor
has struck out once again.

It's getting me real paranoid.
It's causing me neurosis.
Even me lucky rabbit's foot's
gone down with myxomatosis.

The elastic on me underpants
never lasts a week,
it gives a whole new meaning
to dancing cheek to cheek.

I couldn't pick a winner
no matter what I chose.
I couldn't pick a racehorse
I couldn't pick me nose.

In my entire life things have never gone
how they should have ought to,
cos for bloody twenty years I've been
a fucking Leeds supporter!

This is another sporting poem. It's about another hero of mine, Ruby Walsh, possibly one of the greatest steeplechase riders ever. As a little claim to fame, it once got read out by a presenter on Channel 4's Racing Program!

Ruby Gets His Head In Front

You can hear the horse thunder
From Galway up to Nass.
The colours of the jockeys,
Emerald Ireland's sacred grass.

You bet and watch your money
drop in the bookies sack.
But Ruby's got his head in front
and gives the mare a smack.

Some run just for money,
some just for the craic.
But when Ruby has his head in front
You'll get your money back.

County Kildare's bravest son.
His father bred him true.
He won the title at first try,
with Papillon he flew.

Three countries daunting Nationals,
all in the same year.
When Ruby gets his head in front
it'll cost those bookies dear.

From Gowran Park to Sligo,
Fairyhouse right down to Cork,
you can see the bookies swagger,
you can curse them as they talk.

I lost my shirt at Wexford
won it back at Leopardstown
cos Ruby got his head in front
and brought those bookies down.

Some run just for the money,
and some just for the craic.
But when Ruby gets his head in front
You'll get your money back.

Ever since I wrote it in the nineties this poem has featured heavily in my stage act. I suppose it owes a lot to John Lennon's song "Whatever gets you through the night"

Habits

Some people need some killer weed
some people need cocaine
some people need some cactus juice
to purify their brain.

Some people need their vodka
and some need Ecstasy
some people need their acid
to make their minds run free.

Some people need malt whisky
some people need their speed
some people feed their habit
and that's all they'll ever need.

Some people use temazepam
and some use novocaine.
Some people need some uppers
and some downers to ease pain.

Everyone needs something
to make it through the night.
Everyone needs something
to forget all of the shite!

Everyone needs something
to have themselves a ball,
but me I've got this problem,
'cause I fucking need it all.

This is another poem about drugs. This one is a warning. I wrote it way back in the 70's (pre rap days!) after losing one friend too many to drugs.

Mirror Man

Oh mirror man is tall and proud
never seems to talk too loud
always stands out in a crowd
a long ranged man
a travelling man
hop along on his caravan
he'll take you high
he'll take you low
he'll take you where you wanna go
just as long as you don't show
surprise within your eyes

But mirror man he still walks tall
he catches you if you should fall
you find you're going when he calls
it seems as if he walks through walls
but as he jokes and as you smoke
you begin to think that there's no hope
of life outside his mirrors

and he has you caught
and your minds stretched taught
your life slips by without a thought
as long as he never deals you short
you're content to gaze through mirrors

but mirrors seem to look both ways
and there's no change between the daze
and eyes are glazed with a distant haze
as you crawl behind the mirror

and now you're lost
and count the cost
your fingers seem to turn to frost
you realise you've been double crossed
and you shatter all the mirrors

but mirror man he turns away
to pastures new for other prey
walk away don't be urged to play
with all the toys he'll put your way
there's danger in his mirrors.

As I live in Scarborough and work on the seafront I get to see far too many stag and hen parties staggering between The Golden Ball, The Lord Nelson and The Newcastle Packet. For some reason many of them seem to end in tears.

Suzie's Getting Married

Suzie's getting married
She's out upon the town
Wear stockings and suspenders
And a plastic golden crown

Along the street she staggers
Through pubs and clubs and bars
An L-plate stuck upon her back
She really wants a car

A cab to get her out of here
A lift to get her home
To dressing gown and slippers
She just wants to be alone

Where everything is comfortable
Familiar and kind
Now the alcohol has worn away
She wants to change her mind

Her life never really happened
Like she hoped it would
She should have been a model
but she didn't have the looks

She should have gone to college
but she didn't have the books

she should have joined that army
she should have had a life

she could have been a someone
not just anybody's wife

Instead she getting married
And she's out upon the town
Wearing stockings and suspenders
As her tears come falling down.

The concept of war being televised isn't new. I remember seeing the images from the Viet Nam war on the television news almost every night in the 60's. However, it was hammered home as we watched the invasion of Iraq live! Since then things have got worse. Perhaps the constant images of war on our TV has desensitised us to the reality of the horror we are seeing. Anyway that's what this poem is about.

Cosy TV News

Cluster bombs explode the sky
Sit and watch a nation die

Images of hate and war
Via satellite dish and mobile phone

On news at ten and news at six
Watch them as they're blown to bits

Then weather and the local news
A city councillor gives his views

A murder and the football scores
Newborn lambs on the Yorkshire moors

The settle down for Emmerdale
Or a documentary about Whales

But meanwhile in a foreign town
Another buildings crashing down

A car bomb in a market square
Bits of bodies everywhere

But we march to a different beat
Time to turn on Coronation Street.

Again I can't remember when I wrote this. I think it was in the nineties. I do remember performing it live at the Bonding Warehouse in York because it's on video on my web site! Can't really argue with that.

Young Love

"You've got to get me in the mood,"
She said to me one night
You've got to talk me into it
I'm meant to put up a fight
You've got to woo me and charm me
You've got to say you care
You've got to do a damn sight more
than shove your hand up there!

You've got to wine and dine me
and seduce me with your wits
you can't just blow inside me ear
and grab me by the tits

I want it to be proper
I want it to be nice
I want for us to get engaged
and save up for a house

I want to plan me wedding
and start me bottom draw
you can stop drinking with the boys
You can't see then no more

and you can't go to t'match on Saturday
we're going into town
we're off to choose some furniture
and put your money down.

You'll have to buy a decent suit
and get a better job
you'd better smarten up a bit
my dad thinks you're a slob

But meanwhile, for the moment
I really couldn't care
cos now that we've become engaged
you can shove both hands up there!

This was inspired by a song by Dennis Leary. Again I mucked it around a bit to make it more appropriate for me. Over the years I've performed it at many bikers festivals always to a great roar of agreement. I also performed it in front of 4,500 people supporting Suzie Quatro. Now that was a night!

Road Rage

Oh my God what an arse hole, you really are such a prat
you can't go around doing stupid things like that.....

Driving real slow in the really fast lane
driving people behind you really insane

then speeding up as they try to pass you
your exhaust's not the only thing turning the air blue

signalling left when you want to turn right
having no lights on in t'middle of t'night

parking at Tesco's in disabled spaces
while disabled people make angry red faces

weaving through lanes like some drunk in the street
driving round in the summer saying "What about the heat?"

driving at eighty on small country lanes
squashing hedgehogs and rabbits and lollipop ladies

using your mobile as you drive down the road
so full of self-importance your head should explode

filling your tank up with petrol and lead
and driving through lights when they're just turning red

your in-car CD takes up all your attention
your bull bars are just another penis extension

There's only one thing I can say unto you
you're an arse hole......
the world greatest arse hole - Fuck You !

This was written in 1974 in the middle of the three day week, one of several measures introduced in the United Kingdom by the Tory Government to conserve electricity, as its generation was severely restricted by a coal miner's strike. I remember writing it by candlelight in my Harrogate flat, fully supportive of the miners action.

Unemployment

I won't be going down t'mill
tomorrow on the bus
I won't be going anywhere
I'll stay at home and rest
cos I've been made redundant
they don't want no skill no more
just sixteen year old lasses
pushing buttons on t'factory floor

Still lassies got to earn a crust
cos times are hard these days
they said they might retrain us
but I'll never change my ways

I've fettled looms for forty years
since I was just a lad
and although they paid me off quite well
I've never felt so bad

I've nowt to do - I'm fifty two
I'll never work again
no factory will employ you
when they think you're over t'hill

So here I sit by t'fireside
and spit into the flames
I've done me time
but never earned enough to see me gains
I'm cast aside, rejected like
washed up at fifty two
yon mill has sucked me life away
and leaves me, sitting, empty like
with bugger all to do.

This is a poem that owes a lot to a lyric by a brilliant writer called Shel Silverstein. Once again I have mucked it around and put my own spin on it. It was too good an opportunity to miss.

Party

There were couples and trios
and foursomes and more
there were people quite naked
all over the floor

there were people in groups
there were people in batches
there were pyromaniacs
looking for matches

there were fathers and daughters
and sisters with brothers
there were people smearing
themselves up with butter

they all rolled a joint
and all passed the wine
then all kissed each other's
then tried to kissed mine

there were sadists and masochists
lined up in a row
saying please hit me
while the others said no.

there were people with fruit
and some with long tongues
necrophiliac's looking
for any dead ones

There were people with bottles
and people with food
and all of them being
exceedingly rude

there were short ones and fat ones
and bald ones as well
all doing to others as they did unto them
then they swapped round and did it again

When the police burst in at the front
I got out the back pretty sharply
and swore to myself that never again
would I join the conservative party.

I wrote this back in the late 70's well before the banking crash of the early 2000's. It was written as a protest at the bank charges I suddenly found I was paying. Again it seems that over the years nothing has changed.

A Poem For All Our Bank Managers

Dracula sucks less blood than you
you pin striped, tight arsed get,
drawing red lines through all the names
of people in your debt

making your decisions
to whom to lend your cash
then working out the interest
on how much you'll get back

You claim you offer service
that's a bloody joke
how come half the tills are empty
between 12 and 2 o'clock

how come you're only open
when everyone's working hard
trying to earn some money
to pay off your credit cards

your bloody bank makes millions
from small borrowers like me
with interest and charges
and all those hidden fees

You only lend us money
when we are in the black
then as soon as we get overdrawn
you demand we pay it back

When we're overdrawn you write to us
and charge us for the letter
then blitz us daily with junk mail
about how credit makes life better

So on behalf of everyone
dear God please hear our plea
curse Midland, Lloyds and Barclays
Nat West and TSB.

This was written in the mid 90's and since then has always been the start point for my live act. I just love the opening line and in a busy and noisy pub it usually shuts the audience up, if only for them to wonder what the hell it is I'm saying!

Contact Ads

Married man seeks passionate affair
with nymphomaniac amputee.

A couple of swingers from Huddersfield
want another to make three.

A biker bitch from Birmingham
wants sex while her husband looks on.

And a leather clad mistress in Manchester
has a collection of rubber thongs.

A naughty nypho in Nottingham
will send you her dirty knickers.

You can find them all in the contact ads
horny housewives to frustrated vicars.

From people who dress up as nuns
and bang away like rabbits,

they represent a microcosm of
our British bedroom habits.

To Anne Summers parties
where everyone gets pissed.

To people who swap their partners
a change is as good as a wrist.

I went to one of those parties
where you chuck your keys down on the floor,

I ended up with an AA box
on the fucking A64.

This was written for the American Bi-Centennial celebrations way back in the 70's.

A Poem about a Huge Pile of Crap

When Noah built the ark, it were a bit of a rush
paint barely were dry when down came the flood

he loaded the animals in t' hold down below
the zebus and zebras were t' last ones to go

he loaded his family, his friends and his cat
then set off to sail as the thunderstorm cracked

he'd been on his cruise for nearly a week
when his wife suddenly said she could smell a strange reek

Then it suddenly hit him, his face fell agog
he'd totally forgotten to build any bogs

he went down in the hold and the crap was so deep
that some of the animals were growing webbed feet

so he set them to work with their feet and their trunks
piling the shit into a huge smelly lump

by using their heads, and their feet and their necks
they all pushed together and got it on deck

it were such a great lump, the ark almost capsized
but they all pushed together till it fell over t'side

it dropped into the sea with a bloody great splash
then just floated around - this huge pile of crap

it covered the sea like a huge brown oil slick
and everyone said that the smell make them sick

so Noah sailed away and left it to rot
and the huge pile of shit settled on rocks

it stewed and it festered, it got bigger and grew
then Columbus discovered it in 1492.

An old poem written back in the 70's and performed with Arkwright's Ferret. I don't think its seen light of day since. But here it is warts and all.

Hangover

My heart's in San Fransisco
my stomach's down the loo
my liver sits there, on the bedside chair
in a puddle of vindaloo

my mouth tastes like a wrestlers
rammed his jock strap down my throat,
and I don't really want to know
what's caked down the front of my coat

I can't stop the world from spinning
to allow me to get off
I've no idea what I really need
is a shit, or a shave, or a cough.

I'm having such a hard time
keeping body and arsehole together
the world's fallen out of me bottom
my tongue has turned to leather

There's a traffic cone in the corner
that I've never seen before
and a policeman's helmet hanging
from the handle of me door.

I think I must have been drinking
it all went down so fine
but sometime later it came back up
and I lost all track of time

A 3 o'clock this morning
I was sleeping like a log
I woke up in the fireplace
needing a hair of the dog

I must try to cut down drinking
I mustn't get so pissed
last night I tried to lay on t'floor
and went and bloody missed

I think I must stop boozing
I've got to cut it down
but bollocks - I'll start tomorrow
'cos I really need a drink right now!

I suppose this is a bit of a pop at the macho type of stuff spouted by The Daily Mail and Daily Express when it comes to summing up the character of us Brits. But no matter how brave we are we all have our weak points.

Up The Brit's

Us Brit's are a race of Vikings
interbred with Saxon and Celts
We're the race that won the ashes
we're British and we're the best

We beat the French at Agincourt
and won the replay at Waterloo
we stuffed the Spanish Armada
won World Wars One and Two

We built the mightiest Empire
the world has ever seen
and fought through mud and bullets
for our country and our Queen

We've got true grit stuffed up our arse
that's why we've stiff upper lip's
we thrive on pints of bitter
and good old fish and chips

Throughout two thousand years of history
at danger we've faced and laughed
- so how come we're all scared shitless
by a spider in the bath.

This poem was a sort of commission. After a gig a couple came up and asked me to write a poem for them because they were 50 years old and had just got engaged. They were having a bit of a do, had a band booked and asked me along to perform my set, and the new one and enjoy the party. I had a week to write it and as I began, it suddenly dawned on me that pretty soon I would be fifty as well. Hence the poem became a lot more personal. Originally it was called Now We're Pushing Fifty, sadly today its title has had to catch up with me.

Now we're over 60!

Now we're over sixty
we should wear our age with pride.
We've been there and we've done it
and we took it in our stride

We bopped to Little Richard.
With Elvis had our first kiss.
Back row in the movies,
a grope in the one and six

A tanner in the jukebox.
A fiver for your pay.
Riding with Gene Vincent,
on the back of a BSA.

The Beatles brought us Strawberry Fields.
The Stones the Altmont Blues.
And war movies on all TV's
the latest Vietnam news.

One two three four.
we didn't want that fucking war.
But what can a poor boy do,
cos sleepy London Town's no place
for a street fighting man.
Chilly, chilly it's evening time
and Waterloo Sunsets fine.
When I think of all the good times
I have wasted, having good times.

We lost a few along the way
Jimi, Brian & Janis couldn't stay
Tim Buckley and Jim Morrison
sang their song and passed along.

But we who still are standing,
we who still survive,
we've been there and we've done it
we wear our age with pride.

We wear it like a banner.
We are the ones who dare.
We're growing old disgracefully,
We're over sixty now - and we don't care!

Rita really was the queen of York's rock n roll scene. She keeps her age a secret but she's seen and heard them all in her time. She's always liked my act and back in the late 90's when it was her birthday and, along with the York band "Hard Lines", she asked me to do a gig for her. I was proud to be part of her celebration and I wrote this especially for the occasion. God knows how old she is now but hopefully she's still rocking - and long may that continue.

Poem for Rita

She rules the whole scene
she's York's rock 'n roll queen.
She's seen everyone
from stars to has been's.

She started shaking with Gene Vincent
rattled with Marty Wilde
rolled to the Swinging Blue Jeans
she took to dancing in the aisles

she did the twist to Chubby Checker
and jeepstered with T Rex
hopped with Mott the Hoople
to the Eagles she had sex

she glammed up with David Bowie
wore tinsel with The Sweet
got heavy with Led Zepplin
and boogied with Canned Heat

she's boogied with the best of 'em
Thin Lizzy and Status Quo
Play anything by Bad Company
And watch Rita go go go

She knew young Gary Barrett
When he was in short pants
She even knew old Aldo
When he was nobut just a lad

She knew all of the Hard Lines
When they were just soft curves
she joins in all their choruses
she knows all of their words

Our York's a ghost filled City
There are spirits near and far
of Vikings, Normans, Romans,
There's spirits behind Bars

But there's only one that shines out
Like a beacon to us all
And that's the spirit of our Rita
The true spirit of rock 'n roll.

Another one-off special poem. This one is for a great bloke, the Scarborough performer named Jesse Hutchinson who got me off my backside and back into performing again in 2015. This was written to celebrate his five hundredth gig at Scarborough's wonderful Cellars Bar.

Five Hundred Gigs

Five Hundred gigs
All in the same place
Some sort of weird continuum
In both time and space
Everyone is happy with a smile
upon their face
just don't dare to sit
in someone else's place.

Five hundred gigs
Just in Cellars bar
People flock from miles around
By taxi, bus and car
From Bridlington and Whitby
And places so afar
Just to see young Jesse
Play his old guitar

Five hundred gigs
Five thousand broken strings.
A hundred thousand songs
Our Jesses had to sing

Americana, Texacana
Country and western swing
He's even covered Donovan
And that Sunshine Superman thing

Five Hundred gigs
For a treetop flyer
Five hundred gigs
And the bar gets higher
On Monkey Wrench
And Farmers too
Neil Young covers
Just for me and you

Graceland and St Judy's Comet
Boots of Spanish Leather
Winding Wheels and Oxford Town
Fifty Ways To Leave Your Lover
Hearts and Bones, Ophelia
My Sweet Carolina
Crosby Stills and Hutchinson
Nothing could be finer

So thank you Mr Hutchinson
From a grateful cellars crew
Happy Five Hundredth birthday
From all us here, to you.

This dates back to the days of performing alongside Gary Barrett and his band in The Roman Baths pub in York. By the way it's not true. I do give a shit about quite a lot of things.

When things go wrong

When thing screw up
as they usually do

and you have no idea
just what to do

when things go wrong
As they usually will,

And your daily road
Seems all up hill

When you lose your money
On a damn slow horse

Or you lose your job
or you lose your voice

If you life seems hard
And you've lost your way

And there's all those bills
that you have to pay

When funds are low
And debts are high,

When you try to smile
But can only cry

And you really feel
You'd like to quit ....

Don't run to me:
I don't give a shit.

This also dates back to the days of Arkwright's Ferret and the folk clubs around London and the "sarf east". I think the main gist of the words originated from Tom Lehrer, and once again I have mucked it about and put a new ending on it.

Germ

I love my friends and they love me
we're just as happy as we can be
and just to show we really care
what ever one of us get's - we share !

I got it from Agnes
and she got it from Jim
we all agree it must have been
Louise who gave it to him

She got it from Harry
who got it from Marie
and everyone knows Marie
- got it from me !

Max got it from Edith
who gets it every spring
and she got it from Daddy
who gives her everything

she gave it to Daniel
whose Spaniel's got it now
my girlfriends even got it
and I'm still wondering how !

John got it from someone
whom we will never know
at Christmas he passed it onto Joan
beneath the mistletoe

Joan passed it onto Sue
who passed it onto Chris
who seems to have picked it up again
when going for a piss

But I got it from Agnes
or maybe it was Sue
or Milly, or Gilly, or Dilly, or Willy
it doesn't matter who

it might have been down the pub
or at the club or the loo
but if you're the arse that gave me their cold
I hope it comes back to you!

This actually is a true story. When you live in Scarborough you, eventually, get used to the noise the seagulls make especially around the breeding season, honest.

Nightmares

There's nothing really fun about a nightmare
They wake you up in middle of the night
You feel your skin is crawling
And you wait until the morning
And the welcoming dawning
Of days the cold bright light

There's really nothing funny about a nightmare
As you lay awake in t'middle of the night
You experience the shivers
from your spine down to your liver
And your brain all of a dither
As you wonder 'bout the cause of all your fright

You lay awake and listen to the screaming
Of the souls of them that went before
of ancient long lost mariners
sailors, drunks and carriers
so you hide behind the barrier
that is your bedroom door

the cold sweat lasts until the morning
your senses and your mind have all gone dull
so you put an old CD on
then it dawns on you the reason
it's the bloody breeding season
for millions of Scarborough's squawking gulls

Whether you like it or not Facebook has become an important part of our lives. I just wish we used it more responsibly, and before you ask, no I don't want to play bloody Candy Crush!

Facebook

Facebook me
and I'll Facebook you
And we'll keep tracks
Of the things we do
You post pictures
Of all your food
Jokes that are very
Slightly rude
Stuff from 38degrees to sign
And photographs
of your good times
videos of cats that growl
videos of cats that howl
videos of cats that jump
videos of cats that hump
more videos of bloody cats
what the fuck do I want with that?

another photo of your tea
what's all that got to do with me?
and those invites to join in games
the bloody things are all the same
Candy Crush and Bejewelled Blitz
A waste of time
Gets on me tits.
Daily notes and witticisms
All mashed up as altruism
The cutting edge of technology
Reduced to mediocrity
So don't Facebook me and
I won't Facebook you
I'm escaping from this Human zoo.

This is a very current issue, especially in North Yorkshire. I wrote it in the spring of 2016 when against the wishes of many local people North Yorkshire County Council voted in favour of fracking. It was filmed the first time I performed it and since going on YouTube, seems to have gone viral.

Anti-Fracking Poem

Fuckity Fuckity Fuckity Fuck
Sold out by the council to make a quick buck

Fuckity Fuckity Fuckity Fuck
The North Yorkshire Councilors really do suck!

Frackity Frackity Frackity Frack
Once you've ruined the water you can't put it back

Yorkshire Conservatives take Third Energies shilling
Selling out all the people who are against all the drilling

Poison the aquifer, poison the land
All for the sake of a few hundred grand

Bugger the farmers the sheep and the ewes
Bugger the tourist who's here for the views

Conservative councilors in the Government's pay
They'll end up with knighthoods for the votes cast today

Dancing like puppets to Cameron's jigs
Now he's screwed everyone one of us, not just dead pigs

sod conservation and all public wishes
flames up your plug hole when you're doing the dishes

when everything falls down a bloody great crack
They'll be sorry they gave permission to frack

Frackity Frackit Frackitty Frack
Once you've extracted the shale gas you can't put it back

Frackety Frackity Frackity Frick
It's not just the water that's making us sick

Who'll explain to the children
Why the fish are all dead

Who'll explain to the drinkers
Why the waters all red

Who'll explain to the tourists
Who'll all turn away

Why North Yorkshire council
Voted that way

Westminster coffers fill up with gold
But it's our children's birthright they just bought and sold

Frackity Frackity Frackity Frack
Once you've fucked up the country you can't put it back!

Back in the day I was a bit annoyed about the growing use of CCTV. I suppose now we've got use to it. One of those 21st century things we've come to accept. But they could have asked us first.

CCTV

Bloody camera in the street
Watching as we meet and greet
Watching every step we take
Watching every move we make

Making sure we stay in line
Spying on our leisure time
The magic eye up in the sky
Into all our lives does pry

Making sure we're free of crime
No need to dial 999
The force is watching every move
Makes the coppers lives run smooth

Hit those rhythms, hit those beats
Reality TV on the streets
Watching every drink we take
watching every breath we make

Zoom in tight to see our face
Surveillance keeps us in our place
Watching as we take a piss
Watching if we hit and miss

Watching as we have a smoke
Watching if we have a poke
Voyeurism getting rife
Turns us into readers wives

Did they ask us? Did they fuck!
If we minded while they look
Surveillance gets us every time
But it never seems to stop the crime

Looking back I think this was about the financial crash and the ridiculous claim by politicians that we were "all in it together".....really?

Everybody hurts

Everybody has a cross to bear
Everybody wants a bigger share
Everybody has an axe to grind
Everybody wants to change their mind
Everybody ran when the house caught fire
Everybody laughed as the flames went higher
Everybody ducked when the fan went mad
Everybody lost when the deal went bad
Everybody remembered when the times were good
Everybody did what everybody should
Nobody expected the worm to turn
Nobody expected that they'd get burned
Now everybody is looking glum
And everyone's saying that life's no fun
Everybody has a cross to bear
And everybody's saying life's not fair.
Everybody's broke
no money for repairs
Everybody hurts
But nobody cares

I had to write a poem for the millennium. On the actual night I was performing a gig at The Roman Baths with Gary Barrett. A few minutes after the bells of York Minster tolled in the new century I got up and did this.

Millennium Poem

Happy new fucking millennium
Lest drink till we all bloody burst
Let's drink to the future
Let's drink to the past
And prey that things just don't get worse

Happy new fucking millennium
Let's drink to the next thousand years
Let's drink to the hope
Let's drink to the glory
Let's drink to an end to our fears

Happy new fucking millennium
Lets drink to a golden new age
So throw on your glitter
And chuck up 'yer bitter
And drink to us turning a page

Happy new fucking millennium
Let's drink as the big wheel goes round
Let's all stay at home
And not visit the Dome
What a waste of a few million pounds

Happy new fucking millennium
But so far I see nothing has changed
We're still just as poor
National health's at deaths door
and Labours gone fucking deranged

Dad's Army is still on the telly
they still haven't legalised dope
Man U's won the league
The workers still bleed
New Millennium, new Labour – same fucking joke

I'm not sure why or when I wrote this, The only thing I know is that "Suicide Is Painless", the theme tune to the movie "Mash" by Johnny Mandel, has always been a favourite song of mine.

Suicide is Painless

Suicide is painless
if you listen to that song
but I can't go out and shoot myself
cos I haven't got a gun

I can't jump off top a' building
cos I'm really scared of heights
I can't even climb a ladder
without a nosebleed and a fright

I tried drinking some Domestos
but it only killed me germs
I think I'd like to be buried
but I'm really scared of worms

I drank a bottle of Jack Daniels
and took some jagged little pills
but before I got to bedroom
I was feeling really ill

I threw up in the kitchen
I threw up on the floor
I even threw up items
that I'd never seen before

I overdosed on Benoline
but it only cured me cough
and gassings out cos the bills unpaid
and the gas board cut me off

I tried to strangle myself with the phone line
but the number was engaged
I tried to buy some hemlock
But it turned out to be sage

I even tried to crucify myself
but it really didn't matter
Despite being ambidextrous
I always dropped the hammer

Perhaps we shouldn't do less drugs
Perhaps we should do more
Everybody should get stoned
and roll around on t'floor

Everybody should get ripped
and giggle at the curtains
and overdose on pizza
with extra anchovies and gerkins

and finish off with chocolate cake
and a bottle of Newcy brown
and then just lay back grinning
and dig the latest sounds

suicide is painless
if you listen to that song
cos living kills you anyway
unless you do it wrong.

Another poem that could be said to be in the category of kicking against the pricks (Acts 9:5), only not in the biblical sense.

The Golden Prophets

Beware the golden prophets
dead before their time.
Beware the grim faced reapers
who tell us it's a crime.

Beware their representatives
don't sign upon their line.
Remember tigers show their teeth
just before they smile.

Always give a false address
and lie about your age.
Always leaving them waiting
don't let them lock the cage.

Always spoil your paper
never leave a note.
Let them think they're winning
never float their boat.

Always keep them guessing
which way you're going to jump.
Answer questions with more questions
spoil their aces with your trump.

Withhold all co-operation
withhold your sweat and toil.
Don't let them reap your harvest
and leave you with their spoil.

Peaceful protestation.
Civilian unrest.
Uncivil disobedience,
get it off your chest

Kick their arses into touch
make them change their gear.
Make them listen out for you,
make them turn the other ear.

Don't give way to compromise.
Tell them it's no deal.
Look back straight into their eyes,
tell them how you feel.

We all are individuals
not just numbers with no face.
It's time the likes of me and you
won this human race.

I suppose this is a cry against the recent Cameron Government, the rise of austerity and their war on the welfare state.

Evil

There's an evil stalking
through our once proud land
Brought to us by
The voters hand

Now Tory promises
Have turned into sand
It's almost like they
had it all planned

sell it off quickly
sell it off cheap
leave the poor and the vulnerable
to struggle on the heap

broken pledges
broken trust
the people's dreams
have turned to rust

the UK's economy
no longer boom and bust
just more and more austerity
welfare state turned into dust

Eton old boys
high on coke
You couldn't make it up
It's just a fucking joke

They say there isn't any money
For welfare benefits anymore
but there's always cash for weapons
to fight their bloody wars

there's always cash for bonuses
and pay rises for MP's
but bugger all when it comes around
to the likes of you and me

Another new poem. It's not that amazing that her death divided opinion. To some she was a hero, to others, well you know what I mean.

It Wasn't Me

Honest Mate – It wasn't me
You've got hold of the wrong man
I was stood there standing
When the proverbial hit the fan

It's got bugger all to do with me
I wasn't even there
I'd wide eyed and innocent
Do I look as if I care?

I was somewhere else Mil Lord
I've got an alibi
My Barrister will prove it
I never tell a lie

I've got an honest face Mil Lord
I walk an honest mile
And don't believe their lawyers
They're just crocodiles with smiles

"Ding Dong the witch is dead"
I'll admit the tune was in my mind
But I wasn't the first to upload it Facebook
When we heard Margaret Thatcher had died.

Is our bad weather due to global warming? I don't know. What I do know is that it seems to have rained most of the year. You notice this sort of thing when you have a business that depends on tourism.

A poem about the weather (and bloody hell haven't we had a lot of it!)

The bloody weathers gone insane
Nowt but bloody wind and rain
To live round here you need webbed feet
A kayaks just floated down our street

The council have no bloody brains
Claiming cuts have stopped them clearing drains
So the rain comes down and the rivers flood
Homes and businesses filled with mud

Waters rise all over the place
A bridge swept away with hardly a trace
Even David Cameron
has had to show his face

Making excuses, wringing his hands
Reminding us all of his spending plans
Promising this, promising that
Dressed in green wellies, looking a prat

But the Tories ain't gonna pick up the bills
If it rains any more we're gonna need gills

When it happened down south they got billions
Coastal defenses and walls
But due to the cut backs in budgets
As usual we in the North get fuck all.

Back in the day we used to sit around and read stuff like Chariots of The Gods (was God an astronaut?) by Eric Von Dankin and then argue about it until the early hours. This poem is a bit like that.

A Poem on the Meaning Of Life
(A bit heavy but bare with it)

The other night
I lay there thinking
About love and life
And all its meanings

And the more I thought
The more I puzzled
The more I thought
The more I got befuddled

So I looked out the window
At the stars, planets and galaxies
The billions of miles
That my eyes could see

The distance involved
Defied any sums
In those billions of light years
Are we the only ones?

Is there life out there?
Is a god sat in his heaven?
Is there hell out there?
Can there really be a devil?

And then an awful truth
Entered in my head
"It's got bugger all to do with me!" I thought
So I went back to bed.

A poem about laying in bed unable to sleep as your mind turns over the one thousand and one things you have to do, should be doing or have forgotten to do.

Night Surfing

As the water rises higher
And a darkness fills the sky
The brain storm tumbles thoughts
And you hope that tempus flies

You're just night surfing
Night surfing

You're not waving, you are drowning
See the light and see the morn
You're not floating, you are sinking
Try to surface with the dawn

Night surfing
It's just night surfing

Sounds of night fade in the distance
You've made it to the day
You watch another rising sun
Spread its light across the bay

You've been night surfing
Just night surfing

But when another day is done
Clouds of night shut out the light
And bed is just a lonely place
To face the terrors, face the fright

Close your eyes.
Just go night surfing
Night surfing

A lot of my poetry seems to be aimed at politicians and their lack of common sense and empathy with the rest of us. I was under the impression they were put into parliament to represent us and our views. It's now very obvious that once there, no matter how well intentioned, they become a part of their party and are forced to stick to the party line irrespective of the wishes of the general public. With very few exceptions they seem to fall victims to lobbyists and vested interests. It shouldn't be like that.

Politicians

Give them an inch
Or give them a mile
They'll take it away
With a wink and a smile

Take it or leave it
It's not up to you
We're the caged
Not the keepers in this human zoo

Put it down sideways
Put it down straight
Set out your own future
Don't leave it to fate

Don't settle for less
Hold out for some more
Don't let your dreams
Be nailed to the floor

You offer a smile
You deal in good grace
You're rewards not a handshake
But a slap in the face

Time to arise and be counted
Make your voice heard
Don't be downtrodden
Don't be deterred

Don't be defeated
Don't give up the fight
And don't let Westminster
blame us for their shite!

There's a lot of lonely people in this world. I think this poem is about not being afraid to say hello to someone and don't be afraid to ask someone for a date.

Love makes the whirly-go-round

Patrick loves Edith and Ethel loves Bob
Ernest loves Lucy and Alice loves Rob
Elton loves David and Peter Loves Paul
Poor little Gordon has no love at all

Kenneth loves Mary and Beatrix and June
He's up in court for bigamy soon
Marnie loves Derek who's married to Sam
But he's having off with some girl from Japan

Fiona loves Jesus and Margaret her cat
Lily loves firemen, if they wear their hat
Beryl loves roses and Edward loves dope
And Edna? Poor Edna, she just lives in hope!

Russell loves Judith but also loves beer
She's leaving him soon at the end of the year
Andrew loves football he's no time for girls
And Susan loves anything, if she gets pearls

We all need a someone
We all need a mate
So be brave and be bold
Dare to ask for a date.

Yes I'm a cat lover. I have two cats, both of them expert in what I call keyboard dancing. It's like a feline sort of "Riverdance" but only done on your computer keyboard when you are trying to type. Once Churchill described Russia as "a riddle, wrapped in a mystery, inside an enigma.", that's not Russia, that's a cat!

Cat

What the hell's wrong with you now
Cat....

Was the food that I bought
not quite right
Cat...

Or isn't the cushion
placed quite right in the sun?

Or isn't the toy with the bell
any fun?

Is that why you scratched
and took a lump off my thumb?
Cat.....

I spend more on your treats
Than I do when I eat

I push you out of my seat
you just land on your feet

I brush you and comb you
and never get thanks

In exchange you ate
all of my plants

That infestation of fleas
brought me to my knees

Your life is pure comfort
relaxation and ease

I do everything possible
trying to please

So tell me
Why've you just shat
On the mat
Cat......?

Some time ago I found a collection of old family photographs. That event led to this poem.

Photographs

The faces from the photographs
Of someone's yesterday
The faces of a time and age
That long time passed away

And who's the man in uniform
With medals on his chest
With twinkling eye and waxed moustache
Did he die like all the rest?

And who's that fearful lady
all bosoms and no waist
umbrella hanging on her arm
and thunder in her face

and who could be that happy crowd
that's padding by the sea
laughing, splashing, pulling faces
rolled trousers up to knee

and who could be that tearful child
whose face is edged in fear
he looks a bit familiar
is he someone who was dear?

the photographs are faded now
like the old man's memory
and when he slips away so soon
there'll be no one left to see

the brother who was killed in France
the aunt that died unwed
faces from works outings in 1923
and all this time I never knew -
me granddad kept a photograph of me

Despite this poem being about death I suppose it's actually a cry to go out and live life to the full, whilst you can.

A Long Time Dead

There's one sure thing that equals us
whether we're pink or blue.
One sure fact that unites us
no matter what we do.

There's one thing that's inevitable
if you're ten or ninety-five
Cos when the final curtain drops
no one gets out alive

You can earn so much money
that it drops right out yer arse
You can have so little money
that life seems like a farce

You can be a saint or sinner
be evil, good and thrive
It really makes no difference
cos no one gets out alive

Whether Hindu, Muslim, Catholic
Whether Christian, Jew or Jane
Bush Baptist, or fundamentalist
It's all the bloody same

There is no other shore you know
upon the other side
There is no silver lining
there is no silver cloud

When you shuffle off this mortal coil
when the final chords been struck
you never get an encore
you've just run out of luck

There are no second chances
There are no more re-takes
A one-off deal is all you get
so it's better not to fake

Cos living is a cliché
it's all been done before.
Death is the only thing
we got left to live for.

So whatever you feel like doing
better do it straight away
This isn't a rehearsal
there is no better way

Just do what you wanna do
no matter what is said
cos when that fat man sings the song
you're a fucking long time dead.

Yet another angry poem about the way we keep getting pushed around by little tin pot bureaucrats, jobsworths and people who abuse their little bit of power by delighting in making life even more difficult for the rest of us.

Angst

I'm getting fucked off
with being pissed around
by bureaucrats, clerks
and uniformed clowns

by people with badges
people in suites
security guards
with big shiny boots

give em a hat
and security pass
they turn into a twat
and a pain in the ass

inspectors of tax
inspectors of VAT
inspecting this and
inspecting that

faceless officials
officaldoms face
collecting my details
on their database

they've got all our names
in alphabet files
they know all our secrets
they know all our wiles

they know what we want
they know what we do
and they're waiting out there
for me and for you

Identity cards,
electronic tags
Big brother state
is driving me mad

Authority's turning
our freedom to farce
If they more from me
they can all kiss my arse.

This poem had to be here in last position. It is the poem I have finished my live act with ever since it was written in the 70's sprawled on my Finchley flat floor with a friend called Ned Smith. If anyone out there remembers Ned they will know exactly why I was sprawled on the floor. I always dedicate it Sadie, a woman I once loved and lost!

Excitable Sadie

Excitable Sadie,
the inflatable lady
arrived through the post yesterday
so I undid the wrapping
and pulled out the packing
and took her upstairs to play.

I pumped and I pumped
and on her I jumped
I ran my hand through her hair
but I got my watch caught
and pulled her hair taught
and out came a fountain of air.

Well, she let out a fizz
and started to whizz
and shot round and round in the room
she startled the cat
when she shot past the mat
and out of the window she zoomed

So it's goodbye Sadie,
the inflatable lady
the woman I've wanted so long
cos all I've got left
is a bit of left breast
with a label that says "Made in Hong Kong."

Monologues

For years I have enjoyed and been influenced by monologues. The sort of material that Stanley Holloway recorded and performed, stuff like "Albert and The Lion". In my opinion the greatest monologue writer of them all was Marriott Edgar. He was the writer that, as well as creating the famous "Albert Ramsbottom" series for Stanley Holloway, also created the wonderful monologues about "The Battle of Hastings" and "The Magna Carta".

So why am I telling you about this? Well occasionally some of the material I perform are monologues, especially three which I must own up, I didn't write myself. In fact I have no idea who wrote them, when, or where. I can't even remember when I heard them for the first time. I have a feeling that over the years I might have altered them a bit to fit my style of performance. It seems to me that monologues are a bit like traditional folk songs, in that their original writer has been lost to posterity, but the material has been handed down from mouth to mouth as a part of our oral tradition. Hence the next three works are given the dubious credit of "traditional arrangement by Graham Rhodes". Well let's face it, folk artists have been getting away with that one for years. After the first three you will come across my attempts to write in this style. So here goes, a section of monologues. If by any chance after reading this section you find yourself wanting more, try to get hold of a book called "The Stanley Holloway Monologues" - it has some crackers in it.

Johnny & Gertrude

Little Johnny was playing in the garden one day,
playing at cards and dice
when into the garden came little Gert
carrying three white mice

I've got some of them, Johnny said
Gert said, "No you've not !"
He said "I'll bet you a penny stick of Spanish
I've got everything you've got".

So Johnny took off his pullover
and laid his navel bare
as he stood up standing
he said "I bet you ain't got one of them there."

"Oh yes I have !" - she lifted her blouse
"Yes I have" said Gert
"the only difference between mine and yours
is that mine isn't covered in dirt."

So Johnny took off his little trousers
and showed what lay beneath
When Gert saw she hadn't got one
she was overcome with grief

She dropped her mouse, ran into the house
shouting for her mum
she said - "Johnny's got something under his pants
and Mum I haven't got one !"

Ten minutes later she was out of the house
She didn't make a sound.
Little Johnny was jumping, bursting with pride
waving his thingy around.

She said "All right John, I know you've won,
but I don't really mind
Cos my mummy said - "As long as I've one of these,
I can have one of them anytime !"

Jonathan Cooper

When Jonathan Cooper
came home from school
he started to cry, and to cry
he cried and he cried
for nearly three weeks
and his mam started wondering why

"What's matter young John ?"
his mother did say
" have you been caught in the bike shed again
or have you been given the stick
for playing at darts with your pen ?"

"Oh no" Young Jonathan said,
"it's nothing like that
It's all got to do with me willie
we were measuring in showers just after games
and mine were so small it looked silly"

"Right", said his mum
"Down to gypsies we'll go
some of his spells we shall borrow
I reckon he'll make it grow long right away,
you'll be tripping over bugger tomorrow"

Next morning at gypsies
young John showed his complaint
it were certainly nothing to boast
and gypsy at first thought he'd sprouted a worm,
and then he prescribed John, hot toast.

"Hot toast", said his Mam
"Have you gone bloody mad,
it's his willie that's lacking you twit,
why, just look at poor little thing hanging there
at tea time I ate bigger chips."

"It's a common complaint, Mrs Cooper", he said
"and mostly men, don't you know,
but nature has found best cure of them all,
cos hot buttered toast makes them grow".

Next morning at breakfast, young John he came down,
he looked like he'd just seen a ghost,
cos on every plate, and piled up to t'roof,
were hundreds of pieces of toast.

"I can't eat all them, mam" Jonathan said
and his face grew morbid and sad.
"It's all right love, there's only two slices for you,
rest of em's all for your Dad".

Aggie The Elephant

When Joe Dove takes his elephants
out on the road
he makes each one hold fast with its trunk
to the tail of the others walking in front
to stop them from doing a bunk.

There were fifteen in all
and it were rather a job
to get them linked up in a row
but once he had fixed them
he knew they'd hold on
cos an elephant never lets go

Well pace it were set by big uns in front
it were surprising how fast they could stride
and poor little aggie
the one at the back
had to run till she very near cried

They were walking one Sunday
from Blackpool to Crewe
they started at the break of the day
and Joe followed behind
with a bagfull of buns
in case they got hungry on the way.

well they came to a place
where the railway crossed road,
an ungated crossing it were
and Joe wasn't to know the express it were due
the moment they happened on there

They were halfway across when he saw the express
it come racing right down the track
and Joe tried all he could
to make then turn round
but an elephant never turns back

Joe thought if he didn't look sharp
this train looked like spoiling his troupe
so he ran on ahead and waggled his buns
to show them they'd best hurry oop

When they caught sight of buns
they all started to run
they soon got across at this gait
except poor little aggie
the one at the back
she were just one second too late.

Well this train it come tear arsing right down the track
and caught her bum on fair and square
well she bounced off the buffers
and rolled down the track
and lay with her legs in the air.

Joe thought she were dead
when he saw her laid with her head on the line
so he knelt down beside her
put his head on her chest
and asked her to say 99

well she wriggled her trunk
and waggled her tail
to show that she were alive
but she hadn't the strength to say ninety-nine
but she managed a weak "85."

when driver of engine got down from his cab
Joe said here's a right how do you do
to see fifteen elephants ruined for life
by a clumsy big bugger like you

driver said what do you mean ruined for life
there's only one hit as I've seen
Joe said "Ey that's right,
but they held on so tight,
you ripped arse end out of t'other fourteen."

Nelson

One bright sunny day down in Dover
young Nelson was supping his ale
when the landlord called time
he said " weather looks fine
let's take the fleet out for a sail"

"Where shall we sail to?" asked Hardy
as he slowly slid off his bench
and Nelson, being pissed and mischievous
said "Let's go put the wind up the French"

They got half way across t'English Channel
when they saw some French ships on the sea
and Nelson and Hardy being friendly
said "Let's invite them all over for tea."

They got some signal flags run up the mast
despite Nelson missing his eye
and Hardy being colour blind and dyslexic
it was all things considered, a good try

Translated the message read "The cats got the fish"
and this puzzled the French till at last
Hardy struck a match to light up his pipe,
then the sea shook with a very loud blast.

Said Nelson "I've told you about smoking"
"I said it would lead to no good"
and they both looked to port and saw a French boat
explode into fragments of wood.

This turn of events upset the French sailors
and all them on deck made rude signs
and them below decks started loading the guns
and they all called Nelson a swine

Nelson said "Shit!" as he ducked under cover
"I think you've just started a war."
But Hardy had seen t'way things were going
and was trying to get down below

"Zut Alors! Sacre Bleu!" all the French screamed
"Fucking Hell !" Nelson said in reply
Within seconds the scene turned to turmoil
and Nelson got hit in the eye.

So Nelson was wounded in t'battle
he said "Eye eye, what a to do!
I can't stand around here just bleeding
it will frighten and worry the crew".

So he called for his mates Freeman Hardy and Willis
to fetch his red jacket and hood
so the crew wouldn't see he'd been hit like
as the colour would disguise the blood

Then as a mighty explosion
came from another French shell
Nelson shouted to Hardy
"You'd better fetch me brown trousers as well!"

As he sank to the deck he grabbed hold of the neck
of Hardy who just happened by
"Kiss me!" he said with a last gasp
"Bog off !" was old Hardy's reply

And that's how Nelson died at Trafalgar
so Britain can always be free
and we can all travel under the Channel
and have the French over for tea.

King Arthur's Poem

The knights were all long and all grey and all cold
the ladies were right pissed off too
when Arthur rode up into Camelot
saying "Eh up lads, what's the to do."

"Cheer up and we'll go kill a dragon
or go overseas on a quest."
but Lancelot answered "Sod off you old Queen."
and spilt wine over Arthur's mail vest

"Steady on there old chap," said Arthur quite vexed.
"just what's this here all about?"
But Lancelot had such a fit of the sulks
that Merlin gave him a clout.

"Well it's like this," said Lancelot rubbing his ear,
"I've come to ask for me cards,
I can't stand all this being the good guy
I want to be nasty and hard."

"I've got this here yen to be evil
to kill a few peasants and then
rape all the women, burn down their huts,
ride off and then do it again."

At this Arthur turned rather funny
and kicked Lancelot right up the bum
then he gave him a lecture on conduct
and how that sort of thing wasn't done

Then Lancelot's eyes grew mean like and shifty
and his face it turned into a leer
I've already started, "he said with a grin
"Cos I've just gone and bonked Guinevere."

At this news Arthur's face sort of crumbled
He threw down his glove, said "Take that!"
he pulled out his sword and with a flick of his wrist
cut Lancelot's plumes off his hat.

This was a sign of a challenge
and the two planned to meet in the dawn
then Merlin stepped in and said with a grin
"Make it early, 'cos I've got to mow lawn."

They met on the battlefield early
and Arthur at sign of daybreak
took Excaliber out and waved it about,
but it flew from his hands into t'lake

and then an amazing thing happened
this hand it came out of the mere
a voice could be heard saying "Oh you great nerd,
you can't chuck your sword around here."

"And just to serve as a lesson
I'll keep it at t'bottom." It said.
and Arthur stood all agog like
then Lancelot chopped off his head.

When everyone saw what had happened
they all shook their heads and went "Tut!"
and Merlin said "Eee what a bugger!"
and poked Arthur's head with his foot

then Lancelot picked it up gently
and started to run down the lawn
and all of the knights tried to stop him
and that's how rugby was born.

Jesus and The Adulteress

'T was a fine sunny day in Jerusalem
so Jesus and t'lads took a walk
they were working out transubstantiation
and were deeply engrossed in their talk

Then suddenly they turned round a corner
and came up against back of a crowd
who were hooting and shouting and yelling
and weeping and wailing aloud.

"Eh up," said Jesus, "What's all this fuss?"
"What's causing all this ado?"
so he elbowed his way through the people
to the front where he asked, "What's to do?"

When they saw who it was t'crowd turned quiet
and murmured under their breath
"We're here to stone the adulteress,
the one what's been sentenced to death."

At this Jesus turned rather solemn
he looked at the crowd with great dread
then a couple of rocks and a broken half brick
whistled past Jesus's head.

Then Jesus took a step backwards
as he tried to get out of the rush.
"Let them without sin cast the first stone!"
He said, and the crowd fell all silent and hushed

Just then a little old woman
holding a rock over her head
stepped from the crowd with a chuckle
and stoned the adulteress dead.

Jesus looked down at the woman
who developed a small nervous cough.
And in a voice charged with emotion, he said
"Mother, sometimes you right piss me off!"

Uncle Ted and the Genie

Poor Uncle Ted bought a magic lamp
from a car boot sale in Hull
then rubbed it up with Brasso
cos it was looking rather dull

Then just as he was rubbing
it fizzed and went off bang
and stood inside Ted's living room
was this funny fat green man

"I am the Genie of the Lamp!"
it said in a voice like thunder
and Uncle Ted was so surprised
he knocked his teacup over

"I've got three wishes for you Ted."
It continued with a grin
and Uncle Ted just stood there
as the enormity sunk in.

"I'd like to win the football pools
and be a millionaire."
"So be it." said the Genie
and the money did appear

Ted grinned, "I'd like to have a harem."
The Genie gave a frown
but soon nubile young ladies
pulled Uncle's trousers down

And now it was the final wish
and Ted thought long and hard
"I'd like to have a willie
that reaches to the ground."

The Genie gave an evil smile
and Ted a nervous cough
The genie made a magic sign
and Uncle's legs fell off.

Epilogue

So here we are then, we've made it together to the end of the book. No doubt if you've got this far there's a pretty good chance that you've bought it. If you did there's another fair chance that you bought it after seeing me at a gig somewhere or other - so thank you. I hoped you enjoyed both of them.

According to my dictionary the word "Poetry" means the following - 1. literature in metrical form; verse. 2. the art or craft of writing verse. 3. poetic qualities, spirit, or feeling in anything. 4. anything resembling poetry in rhythm, beauty etc. Now it strikes me that's a pretty wide definition and that's how it should be.

To me poetry not only includes the words and works of such well-known writers as Betjeman, Robert W Service, Coleridge, McGough, T.S. Eliot, Hardy and both Dylan's (Thomas and Bob), but other people. Lyric writers such as John Lennon, Jimmy Webb, Paul Simon, Roy Harper, Robyn Hitchcock, Michael Stipe, John Sebastian, Tom Rush, Noel Gallagher, and many, many others too numerous to mention - so how come we were never told that at school? How come they rammed stuff down our throats that was guaranteed to put us off poetry for the next lifetime?

People's attitudes, especially those people who stage gigs, have been tainted by this hang-over of misconception. The number of times I've tried to get gigs in pub's and rock venues only to be told things like - "We don't do poetry here, the audience won't like it." "Poetry!

Oh that won't go down here." "Our audience don't want stuff like that here!" Hey, well guess what, a lot of them do! As proved by pub venues like Fibbers, The Roman Baths, The White Swan, The Pavilion Vaults, Cellars Bar and The Merchant.

For over forty years now I've done my own brand of poetry in pubs, clubs, festivals, theatres, biker rallies, folk clubs, village halls, and Selfridges! Everywhere with the exception of the ubiquitous bar mitzvah's and fish fryers suppers. I've worked on the same bills as blues bands, rock bands, indie bands, rap bands, covers bands, local bands, metal bands, acoustic bands and some famous acts like John Otway, Half Man Half Biscuit, Credit to the Nation, Toby Jepson, The Animals, John Cooper Clarke, Suzie Quatro and many more.

In my experience audiences don't mind poetry, in some cases they even quite like it. So the next time you see the word "poet" on the bill don't walk by, don't put up the mental burning cross. Take a gamble, try it for yourself, you just might find you enjoy it.

Till we meet again –

Graham Rhodes
Scarborough 2016

About the author

Graham Rhodes has over 40 years experience in writing scripts, plays, books, articles, and creative outlines. He has created concepts and scripts for broadcast television, audio-visual presentations, computer games, film & video productions, web sites, audio-tape, interactive laser-disc, CD-ROM, animations, conferences, multi-media presentations and theatres. He has created specialised scripts for major corporate clients such as Coca-Cola, British Aerospace, British Rail, The Co-operative Bank, Bass, Yorkshire Water, York City Council, Provident Finance, Yorkshire Forward, among many others. His knowledge of history helped in the creation of heritage based programs seen in museums and visitor centres throughout the country. They include The Merseyside Museum, The Jorvik Viking Centre, The Scottish Museum of Antiquities, & The Bar Convent Museum of Church History.

He has written scripts for two broadcast television documentaries, a Yorkshire Television religious series and a Beatrix potter Documentary for Chameleon Films and has written three film scripts, The Rebel Buccaneer, William and Harold 1066, and Rescue (A story of the Whitby Lifeboat) all currently looking for an interested party.

His stage plays have performed in small venues and pubs throughout Yorkshire. "Rambling Boy" was staged at Newcastle's Live Theatre in 2003, starring Newcastle musician Martin Stephenson, whilst "Chasing the Hard-Backed, Black Beetle" won the best drama award at the Northern Stage of the All England Theatre Festival and was performed at the Ilkley Literature Festival. Other work has received staged readings at The West Yorkshire Playhouse, been shortlisted at the Drama Association of Wales, and at the Liverpool Lesbian and Gay Film Festival.

He also wrote dialogue and story lines for THQ, one of America's biggest games companies, for "X-Beyond the Frontier" and "Yager" both winners of European Game of the Year Awards, and wrote the dialogue for Alan Hanson's Football Game (Codemasters) and many others. You can find out more at his website http://www.grahamrhodes.com

Other books by Graham Rhodes

"Footprints in the Mud of Time,
The Alternative Story of York"

"The York Sketch Book."
(a book of his drawings)

"The Jazz Detective."
(a detective story set in 1950's Soho)

The Agnes the Witch Series

"A Witch, Her Cat and a Pirate."

"A Witch, Her Cat and the Ship Wreckers."

"A Witch, Her Cat and the Demon Dogs"

"A Witch, Her Cat and a Viking Hoard (In preparation)

Photographic Books

"A Visual History of York."

"Leeds Visible History"

"Harbourside - Scarborough Harbour"
(A book of photographs available via Blurb)

"Lost Bicycles"
(A book of photographs of deserted and lost bicycles available via Blurb)

"Trains of the North Yorkshire Moors"
(A Book of photographs of the engines of the NYMR available via Blurb)

Printed in Great Britain
by Amazon